Wild

Laura Lee Tanner

BookLeaf
Publishing

India | USA | UK

Presentation by *BookLeaf Publishing*

Web: www.bookleafpub.com

E-mail: info@bookleafpub.com

ISBN: 9789358313277

First edition 2023

*I would like to dedicate this to my Father,
Raymond Tanner, whose last words of
wisdom to me were, 'Live simply.'*

PREFACE

I have come to the conclusion that my favourite place to dwell is in the here and now. The simplicity of noticing each season, or time of day, holds a certain beauty which is not restricted to scenes we would consider pleasing.

I love to find the magic in small things wherever I am, be that a chestnut wood or the brutalist confines of a shopping centre; to appreciate something, no matter how small, in every moment.

This collection of poems is simply a set of observations, or reflections, on things as they present themselves, whether that be an object, place, time or concept.

Starting

I sit, snow-blind
At the centre of the page
At the edge of the void
Waiting to fall
Waiting to trust that, in falling
I will encounter form, and find within it
A tangible platform on which to build
Layers of creation
Flickering and dancing into life
Within the stillness
Of the Mind's Eye

Tea

The sudden fizz of a kettle about to boil
Triggers a thirst, as yet unrecognised
Now sharpened by a bird-shrill whistle
And the clink of fairy chimes
By the fusion of thick-handled china
And coiling steam
Now quenched by an inward-rushing tide
Of liquid heat, air and astringency
An alchemical moment
Woven into the fabric of the day

Shopping Centre

Autumn mist wreathes dead concrete
Where crows gather
And fountains of luminous red
And yellow leaves
Pop through the gloom

A girl puts out tables and chairs
Bare metal scraping the morning silence
Soft footsteps on cold paving slabs

She approaches a huddled figure
Cocooned in blankets
Carefully placing a hot drink beside the
Makeshift nest

Above, crows watch and wait
Guarding their spiky homes of dark sticks
High in the skeleton hands of trees

Wild

Run like a deer
Through the dappled chestnut woods
Crashing through hedge and thicket into
The open world beyond
Where white skies stretch wide
And your sinews stretch to take the flaxen
Stubble of fields in your cloven stride
Run wild in the morning dew
Air crisp as an apple and dank with decay
Towards the low, pale Winter sun
And beyond
Into dreams of Spring

January Yellows

It's not that I want you gone
Though it seems I'm tired of you going on
Be sure I love you just the same
As any other month by any other name

And when I'm wrapped up warm inside
It's not from your golden gaze I'm trying to hide
I'm contemplating what's in front
And what's behind me
In this time

I see golden Winter sunshine
Light on the water
And the icy glow of frost and snow
From wide and empty skies

When I remember
To stop in the moment
I realise how beautiful you are;
How beautiful you are in your naked Winter
Light playing through your hair

And when I'm wrapped up warm inside
It's not from your golden gaze I'm trying to hide
I'm contemplating what's in front
And what's behind me
In this life

I see golden Winter sunshine
Light on the water
And the icy glow of frost and snow
From wide and empty skies

When I remember
To stop in the moment
I realise how beautiful you are
How beautiful you are in your naked Winter
Frost settled in your hair

Cycles

The year turns
Slowly like the Earth
It's movement almost imperceptible
But irresistible; a gentle force
Compelling trees and creatures to sleep
In a twilight world, slowed and subdued
A pregnant pause…
Or so it seems

As all is alive within;
The spark in all living things
Glowing patiently in anticipation
Of change on the wings of a stirring breeze
Compelled now to jump up and dance
In flames of unfettered joy

Before returning
Once more
To sleep

Light

This poem has 2 versions:

In the first, each statement is presented in a spectrum of concepts from the physical to the cerebral.

In the second, ideas are represented by the first letters of the colours in the physical spectrum which forms visible light.

1.

A spectrum of frequency perceived by our
sensory organs
The catalyst for life as we know it
Containing everything in it's singular potential
The simple permission to exist
The Genesis code
Our innate being
Fundamental truth
Joy made visible
Source
Home

2.

(Infra-red)
Invisible made visible
(Red)
Realised potential
(Orange)
Our Divine nature
(Yellow)
Your ultimate destination
(Green)
Genesis code; God
(Blue)
Breakthrough
(Indigo)
Innate wisdom
(Violet)
Visible joy
(Ultra-violet)
Universal law

Spring Song

In a quiet space
Merging into green
Home is in this place
Cradled by the trees

Nestled here below
On the water, slow
Friends are passing by
Laughing as they fly

Put another log upon the fire
While outside the trees are towering high
Trees and banks are green outside my window
Just sitting, gazing
I can watch the grass grow

Movement

Keep moving!
Don't let the damp creep of inertia
Find a way in
Setting muscles and bones;
Minds and dreams
Into fossils you no longer remember how to use;
Too atrophied to recall the freedom
Of movement
Fluidity
The effortless flow
Of one foot in front of the other
One day
One thought
One action becoming the next
In a timeless, cascading dance

Important People

I have to say
(I hope you know)
That I will miss you
If you go

Our lives upon this earth are short
So for our loved ones, give a thought
Or better still, a warm 'Hello'
A hug, a 'Thank you'
So they know

How much we value what they bring
To every day - the little things
Their stories varied; rich, unique
Each one a treasure, ours to keep

For even when the journey ends
They still remain
Forever friends

Commute

What time is it?
Have I been asleep?
What happened while I was sleeping?
Is there anybody?

On the move - on the tracks
Looking forward, looking back
Front to front
Back to back

Making patterns on the day
On the windows, in the rain
Looking forward, no expression
As we've done for a million days

Keep dreaming
Keep holding on
We keep feeling
But no-one ever knows
On the surface; on the inside

What time is it?
What happens when I die?
Is there some way I could be living?
Am I anybody?

Moving on - on the tracks
Crossing over, crossing back
Side to side
Front to back
In our separateness

Making patterns on the night
On the darkness
In the light
Looking forward, no expression
As we've done a million times

Keep dreaming
Keep holding on
We keep feeling
But no-one ever knows
On the surface; on the inside

What time is it?
Am I still asleep?
What is this madness we are living?
Is there anybody?

Morning

The morning creeps across the window
As I sleep
And, begrudgingly, I open my eyes
To the beauty outside

It always takes a little time to face the day
But the sun assures me things will be okay
Everything will be okay

I love the Autumn leaves
I like my coffee strong
The kettle whistles
As I play my morning song

The leaves are falling down
All brown and gold and red
The river holds me
As I put myself to bed

And when I wake
I see the places that I know
And it seems there's not
Much further to go

For I have travelled for
Three-hundred river miles
Through the meadows and the valleys I have
roamed
But it feels like coming home
It feels like coming home

The May

The light in the morning spreads over the fields
And over the flocks, with their lambs so new
The sun is lifting the dew from the meadow
Adorning the flowers with precious jewels

So sing for the sunrise, and sing for the morning
Sing like a lark in the sky so blue
The May is blooming - a new day is dawning
A day in the Springtime of life anew

An echo is sounding deep down in the forest
The season is turning beneath the trees
The Earth, she is stirring -
Awaking from slumber
Her mantle becoming a cloak of green

So sing for the sunrise, and sing for the morning
Sing like a lark in the sky so blue
The May is blooming - a new day is dawning
A day in the Springtime of life anew

The music is playing; the pipers are piping
And children are dancing around the tree
Our voices are joining the birds in the chorus
Along with bright ribbons, all flying free

So sing for the sunrise, and sing for the morning
Sing like a lark in the sky so blue
The May is blooming - a new day is dawning
A day in the Springtime of life anew

Hope

My hope is like a mushroom
Somebody said to me
Rising up from deep within
If only you could see

From tiny spores to forest floors
It started long ago
And in the dark, whilst I did toil
In secret it did grow

It has become so very large
No longer can it hide
The forest it has now outgrown
And seeks to break outside

It sees the path
It feels the wind
On which new lands are blown
We step outside, my hope and I
Into the great Unknown

(Dedicated to Luisa Herculano)

The Wild Wood

Take me to the Wild Wood
It's promise brooding, dark upon the horizon.
I long to enter the hallowed, leafy halls within
And burrow beneath the tangled roots below

To hide in a womb of earth and moss
Until the leaves become my hair
And bark, my skin;
Fingers and toes spreading like roots;
Uncurling like ferns

Take me to the Wild Wood
Where my very core transforms into glowing
heartwood
And the mycelium of my nerves and veins
Extends and and connects me
To a whispering network of ancient language

Take me to the Wild Wood
And leave me there;
To weather with the ages,
And mould into the soft contours of the earth
Until we are One

(For Laura Taylor)

Zero Point

A place where the path meets the horizon
The space between breaths
A point of pure potential
A pinprick of light
An empty space
Devoid of fear
Devoid of judgement

(For Dierdre)

The Lillies On The Ice/A Winter Voyage

In the bright stillness of a mist-hushed morning
Watched only by a heron, still graceful in his
tattered coat
We churn thick, brown river bed
Striving for deeper water, which breaks
Into syrupy ripples around my Ark's heavy hull

As we pass, the heron takes flight
With a prehistoric cry
Wings beating against the Sun's pale halo
Hung low in a glass-grey sky

Shapes loom among ephemeral reeds
Overhung with damp black branches
And sudden twists and turns appear
As surprising as the silver flash of a fish
Among dark, trailing weeds

A safe harbour calls in the fading light
And the cold closes in around our dock
Wind shrieks through steel girders
And a solitary light shines out into the night
From the dark mass of a tower block

The river thickens around us
It's living molecules squeaking and hissing
As they slowly turn to ice
Wrapping us in a Wintry embrace
And my Ark's hull in a gentle vice

At last, the long hours of darkness behind,
We emerge from our cocoon of night
A new dawn reveals, hard, glinting beauty
Glittering in the morning light

And there, lie lillies!
Scattered upon the ice
Their radiant blooms glowing stark
Against Nature and industry's canvas
A fragile, ethereal
Sign of life

Irises

The tender shoots of Springtime
Emerge from earthy beds
Their beauty hidden till the time
They raise their splendid heads

These gentle spears of brightest green
In reaching for the light
Represent a new beginning
A page on which to write

The long, crisp buds
Which, fold on fold
Contain such power within
Await their cue to open wide
Warmed by the light of Spring

Their vigour and tenacity
Inspires the same in me;
Reminds me of my inner strength
And capability

In softest darkest purple
A regal, velvet gown
With searing golden comet
In the centre as it's crown

This noble flower, to me
Represents a miracle
A lighthouse in the darkness
An empty void made full

(For Wendy & Phil)

Carreg Clochdy (Llyn Brianne)

In deepest, darkest Wales at dusk
The silence seems expectant.
It hums with the air of a question
About to be asked...

The utter darkness of nightfall
Is a blank canvas for the mind's eye
To project all sorts of imaginary
Lights and patterns upon

It is like being back in the womb, or in space
With no sense of time or place
But the slow forming of a question...
"What now?"

Father

Sometimes I don't believe it
It surely can't be true
That I must live the rest of my life on Earth
Without you

The World with you in it made sense
We shared a common view
You said I was your teacher
But you taught me all I knew

So wonderful it was to spend
Those years, those hours with you
So effortless; companionable
So loving, kind and true

It seems unreal to think
That I won't speak with you again
I like to think somehow we might
Upon another plane

For what is death?
And what is real?
As, when I see your face
In photographs, it's love I feel
And that still has it's place

And I can still be happy
In that space and time we shared
As real now as it ever was
Because I know you cared

Gratitude

My heart is full to bursting
As if the whole Sun were within my chest
Radiating outwards for miles and miles
A beacon stretching beyond the sky

I look upon my life; my home
My treasured memories with burning joy
Surely there is no other soul
Who feels as fortunate as I

This state of mind sustains me
Through times both lean and fair
As tangible as gold
My Bread of Life, I gladly share